HANDBOOK
FOR WEEKEND DADS

...and anytime grandparents

60 POWERFUL THINGS DAD CAN DO FOR
QUALITY TIMES & HAPPY MEMORIES

Pete

JEROME MARK ANTIL

ISBN: 1453724885
ISBN-13: 9781453724880
Library of Congress Control Number:
2010911092

A VISITATION HANDBOOK

Separation or divorce, when any children, but especially very young children are involved, can be debilitating – and I'm not going to dwell on it. This guide is some of how I was able to grapple through it – I hope it helps you.

Jerome Mark Antil

For
Lauren Elizabeth

INTRODUCTION

If you're a father, in the midst of the stress a separation or divorce proceedings can cause, this "Introduction" was written especially for you. If you're not going through it, but you are a father, other family member or caretaker, you may find it useful, as well.

Dad, I don't care what your lot in life is, I don't care what you're going through emotionally and I don't care what anyone is saying about you. I don't care if you're right or you're wrong. I don't care if you're happily married or are going through stages of the deep pains and depressions of a divorce and are miserable. There are a couple of facts I just want you to etch in your brain and they are:

1. More than 75% of childhood suicides happen in fatherless homes.
2. More than 90% of homeless runaways happen in fatherless homes.

Wherever you or your head are at this very moment in time – do not forsake your kids. Fatherless doesn't always mean not physically being there with them – although that is important – fatherless is not being there for them at all – emotionally. That's what matters. Visits are so important, of course – but do something, anything. Make phone calls, write letters. Make regular contact with your children. Do anything you can do to reach out to your children and to stay in touch, every day, every week, as often as you can. Their whole world deals in moments. They desperately need to hear from their Dad. It can fill a lot of moments for them. They need a Dad in their lives. Don't run away.

IT'S THE LAW!

And if you're being pushed away – go to court – they will not tolerate it.

YOU ARE ALWAYS DAD!

No matter what you may think in your depression - a Daddy is a star in the eyes and heart of every child on earth - don't ever let anyone tell you otherwise.

A PROMISE TO A 13 YEAR OLD...

All I hope to do with this simple little book, written from my heart - is to help that star shine a little brighter from time to time just by sharing some hints of things that worked for me, when I went through it.

I made a promise to my child that I would share the ideas that worked for us, with other dads, like you. The order you are reading the ideas in is the order in which I wrote them. I will never forget going through a very rough time – and surviving it – and I didn't survive it thinking in order. I did it one visitation at a time.

You will too.

This is probably one of the shortest books in history, my *Handbook for Weekend Dads*, but consider it my "Gettysburg Address" to dads I can identify with. Lincoln wrote his on the back of an envelope and it inspired a nation. I hope this "Survival Guide" inspires Dads to stay strong while it gives them some ideas that may help during these times.

I'm not a Doctor or a Therapist – I'm just a Dad – like you. I know how emotionally tough being a weekend Dad can be at times, especially in the early days of these changes in your life.

FIRST THINGS FIRST.

Let's set the record straight.

"Weekend Dad" is a term someone made up once. Never ever forget that you are just plain Dad. Now, and forever. Not only for real but for always, especially in the hearts and minds of the kiddos. Not for one minute will a child forget or stop loving their Dad.

You never have a reason to be insecure about that. Get it out of your mind.

There are some suggestions I can make from my own experience for when you have the kids for either a routine visitation or for just a surprise visit.

Regardless of where your head is at the moment – never once forget that they truly do want to be with you, and they want to see you and just have a great time with a good healthy blend of fun and quality togetherness with their Dad – and Grandparents too.

THEY DON'T WANT MUCH

Kids love a bit of independence, but they even love security more, knowing that they can trust "you" to be there for them. Try to leave the "stressed" you outside the door – at least during the visit. There are a blue zillion reasons we all are where we are in life that kids had nothing to do with. Try to step out of your head for the time they are going to be with you, and know that you are about to contribute to a lifetime of memories that you all will share as you all look back – from another time in the future.

I know it is sometimes hard to believe – but, whatever happens to be going on in your life, "this too shall pass."

Hey, you are their Dad! Nothing will ever change that.

Put that game face on, step up to the plate and get ready to play ball!

LET'S BEGIN!

Kids have wonderfully simple minds – try not to complicate them.

My daughter was almost five when our visitations started and I began telling and reading her bedtime stories and the stories she remembered most, still capture her imagination as fond childhood memories of time with her daddy, and stories he told or read to her.

Here are some helpful "visitation" ideas I want to share from my own experience.

Idea 1
Kids like reliable routine. It comforts them.

If you think about it – don't we all? They like to know they are secure. I found a familiarity in routine helps them attain that comfort – even if they are going back and forth between parents. Find the one, two or three routines you can do religiously every time you are together – just to help them get their bearings. Think it through – don't over complicate it. Don't ask, just do it – make it a routine.

For several years I would drive 5 hours to get my daughter. It would be a 5 hour drive back to my house, and we usually pulled into town about 11PM. Even if she had dozed off on the way back, I would gently awake her as we came into town so she could see things familiar to her. We always stopped at a nice 24 hour grocery to get a few important items for the weekend. Her chore was to go pick out and get a plastic bottle of milk. (Never out of my eyesight, of course...but it did give her a sense of responsibility, and also it was a routine she was comfortable doing and very familiar with having done it each time she came to town)I would get eggs and a couple more things I already knew I wanted, and we were back in our car and then just a few minutes from home and a wonderful visit.

As she got older, she would get the milk and some other things including some magazines for her – but always the same store – always the same order of events – always a reliable routine she could count on.

Your routine could be something unique to you. Just come up with something so when they are old and gray they will be telling their grandkids –"I used to love to go see my Dad - I remember we would always..."

I don't care how trivial the routine is – it will be the routine with their Dad they will remember, and they will associate it with the quality time they spend with you.

Idea 2

Make a statement early that this visit is about quality time – it isn't about sitting around and watching television or being stuck at computers playing games, or sleeping late – by anyone – Daddy included. I would take all the cell phones – including yours – turn them off and put them in a drawer.

This is the time when everyone spends time together with no distractions.

A GREAT START

One thing I did – which was very easy and never failed to bring a happy smile and started things off with the statement that this whole time was going to be about quality time – was a very simple treasure hunt.

I would take a pad of "post it" notes (if you have more than one - consider a different color for each child) and write clues on them (different clues for each child). "Look under your pillow" or "Look in the top drawer in the bathroom" or "Look under the left sofa cushion" --- of course you would place the clues where you would say to pick up the next one. This makes it easy for you. Try six or eight clues. The starter clue can be just inside the door or on the kitchen counter, and whatever it says is the first place you hide one. What you wrote on that one would be the second place and so on. I also suggest that you fold each note down a couple of times. This takes a little more effort and involvement on their part and adds to the fun. At the final destination you can have a small gift – or it can be some money they use during their visit with you – or it can even be a note to get a good night's sleep because tomorrow you're all going to the zoo or a movie or to something special.

The treasure hunt was always a good ice breaker for me. It set the tone right as we walked into the door that this visit wasn't about me and it wasn't about my child – it was about us...and us takes a little more time and effort and patience.

It's also another routine they will recall fondly every time they think of their visit with you.

Idea 3

Try to make breakfast in the morning – every morning - where everyone sits at the table at the same time. No matter how long or how short a breakfast it is – it's a nice message that "My Daddy made breakfast."

"JERECAKES" BECOME YOUR INVENTION.

This is a perfect time to try my world famous (in my own mind) "alphabet" or "full name" pancakes.

1. Make or buy pancake batter, eggs and cooking oil. (Pancake batter takes seconds to make).
2. Heat the pan *slowly* with a low heat – *never quickly*. I spray it with Pam first or put a tablespoon of cooking oil on it and rub it all over the surface with a paper towel. You want it oiled but not running in oil. When pan is ready, a drop, of water will ball up and roll around on it.
3. Get a big empty plastic syrup bottle (make sure it's one with a spout on top)

and fill it with pancake batter and put the *nozzle* top back on. (You get an empty one by buying a big full one and emptying it into a bowl or jar.) Small sacrifice for the fun it will bring.

4. After you fill the empty syrup bottle with your pancake batter, you are about to become a chef *artiste extraordinaire*.

5. Now make *"alphabet"* pancakes – do your children's names one letter at a time (more letters if you have more room on the pan) – or – when you get really good you could write their names into one pancake. I promise you this is fun, and it will keep them at the table the whole time, with their hero.

Making breakfast is an easy and enjoyable experience – but a routine that can leave a lasting bond. I never worried about what to put on my child's plate. I did the buffet approach. I just put some fruit (whole or sliced) on one plate –a few strips of bacon or sausage on another and some buttered toast or toasted English muffin on still another plate. I put the plates in the middle of the table, all within reach to be shared. This made our breakfast buffet open to each person's own tastes for the morning. Always a full glass of OJ each though. I think you will find the "alphabet" or "name" pancakes a hit, and it can become a standard during each visit. Even eggs made to order will be a great start.

Idea 4

This can be an important thing for you to consider. It is a look at a child's world through their eyes – and this can be helpful to you in creating quality time.

By the way – quality time can be every single minute you are all together. When I was driving my daughter, we would play many games, but one popular one was the *alphabet billboard* or *sign game*. Whoever went first had to find a word on a sign or billboard that started with the letter "A" – then the next person had to find a word beginning with a "B" and so on. This was a great deal of fun and passed the time away with quality, some fun and some laughs. You can also play it looking for the numbers one through nine.

...now consider this.

CELEBRATIONS!

As adults we think in terms of seconds-minutes, hours-days, weeks-months, seasons-years, day-night, weekdays-weekends and pay days.

Am I right?

Kids think in terms of "celebration" like Valentine's Day and Easter, summer and Halloween, Thanksgiving and Christmas, Birthdays and Tooth Fairies, Mommy – Daddy, Grannies – Grandpas, and swimming.

Am I right?

It doesn't get much more complicated than that - and if you want to keep it simple and quality at the same time – get out your calendar, mark every month with one or more of the "celebrations" for the kids, and write it on every visitation date for the month or so leading up to the "celebration."

The same "celebration" can appear on more than one month. Kids never lose their interest in a "celebration" and every time they come to visit you can do something completely different celebrating the very same event.

As an example – Halloween – one visit before the holiday, you can draw and cut out pumpkin designs or Halloween black cats from colored paper and hang them on your refrigerator or some special place.

On another visit, you could make Halloween cookies (I'll show you how later). On still another, you could go find a pumpkin patch or pumpkins at a store and bring them home and carve them. And so on...right up until Halloween.

DOESN'T MATTER WHO GETS THEM

It doesn't matter where children are or which parent they are with on the actual day of the event – your "quality time" visits before the event will become *lasting memories* of that celebration for them and for you.

This "stretching" of a celebration will work with any holiday or celebration, as their interest will not diminish – only heighten. Just come up with something that is both simple and creative each visit - something that will make really *good quality time together*.

If they have friends in your neighborhood, you could include them as well. I will show you a pre made cookie mix so simple all you have to do is roll it out and cookie cutter it (shapes appropriate for the season or event, of course), bake a dozen or so minutes, and be a *hero for life*! Your helper cuts the cookies and puts the sprinkles on, of course.

Have more than one helper? Then it's the pan of cookies each challenge.

Think about all the events in their lives. Write them on the calendar - plan them in advance – and all will go smoothly and be a wonderful surprise for them providing lasting memories. You don't have to out impress anyone or out spend anyone – you just have to remember. Remembering is bigger than any pocketbook - and will make a special moment for them.

½ pound softened butter
1 ½ cups sugar (granulated)
½ teaspoon baking soda
¼ teaspoon salt
2 eggs
2 ½ cups all purpose flour
1 teaspoon vanilla

In a large bowl mix the butter, salt, sugar and baking soda. Mix with beater or mixing spoon for three minutes. Blend in the eggs and vanilla. Add the flour slowly while mixing.

Chill in refrigerator for a couple of hours. Then throw some flour on a surface –you're your rolling pin and roll it out and have fun with the cookie cutters.

Bake on a cookie sheet (no oil on it) in a *preheated* oven at 375* for 10 to 12 minutes.

You could make the cookie dough before the visitation.

TAKE PICTURES EVERY VISIT

Do not forget to shoot pictures all through
the visit – as well. (AND MAKE PRINTS)

Here's an easy way to remember what your
alternatives for in-home fun can be.   Think in
the simple terms of "cookies" or "paper cutouts."   Do one or the other, for the young.
Story reading, of course – always, (Even make
stories up).

Start by going to some stores that sell baking utensils. You will need 2 cookie sheets –
one or two cookie cutters for each holiday
and a rolling pin and large mixing bowl and
spoon. While you're in a store buy several different colors of sugar sprinkles. I promise you
that this is not difficult and can make many
years of smiles and happy memories.

PLANNING THE CELEBRATIONS!

January
Start celebrating Groundhog Day (Go to
the Zoo) Too cold? (Visit some pet stores –
pretend they're a zoo – but no buying) (Go
to a park and take pictures of animals – birds
and squirrels)

Prepare for Valentine Day(Bake heart
shaped cookies one time) (Drawing paper

heart cutouts another time) (Learn to Dance)

February
Start celebrating Valentine Day(Bake cookie hearts one time) (Drawing paper heart cutouts another time) (Learn to Dance) (buy and mail Valentine cards)

March
Start celebrating St. Patrick's Day(Bake cookie shamrocks – with a green food coloring in dough one time) (Shamrock paper cutouts another time)

Start celebrating Easter(Bake cookie Easter eggs one time) (Cookie Easter Bunnies another time)

April
More Easter(Bake cookie Easter eggs) (Bake cookie Easter Bunnies) (Easter egg coloring) (Easter egg decoration cutouts)(bowling, fishing)

May
Start celebrating Mother's day (C'mon – be a hero – help design card – wrap a gift – from them not you) (bowling, fishing)

June
Start celebrating Father's day - Let someone make breakfast and give their Daddy breakfast in bed. (Baseball games) (bowling, fishing)

4th of July Draw and color flags – Put out a flag. Find a picnic or fireworks display.

July
Picnics – Swimming – Library visits – Fishing – Croquet – Zoo – Baseball games – July 4th fireworks shows – museums. (Baseball games) (bowling, fishing)

August
Picnics – Swimming – Library visits – Fishing – Croquet – Zoo – Baseball games – museums. (Baseball games) (bowling, fishing)

September
Start celebrating Pre Halloween(Bake cookie pumpkins and Halloween cookie shapes) (or Halloween paper cutouts) (Baseball games) (bowling, fishing)

October
Start celebrating Halloween(Cookie pumpkins and Halloween cookie shapes) (paper pumpkin and cat cutouts) (Go to a pumpkin lot and get pumpkins to carve)

Start celebrating Pre Thanksgiving(Cookie holiday shapes – Christmas or Pilgrim hats) (Paper cutouts)

Decorate a "Family Christmas table tree – with decorations drawn, colored and cut out.

November
Start celebrating Thanksgiving(Bake cookie holiday shapes – Christmas or Pilgrim hats) (Paper cutouts) (Put up a small Christmas tree – and start decorating with cutouts (and lights)

Start celebrating Christmas(Bake cookie Holiday shapes – Christmas stars and candy canes and snowmen) (paper cutouts)

December
(Cookie Holiday shapes – Christmas stars and candy canes and snowmen, paper cutouts)

Idea 5

BEDS GET WET

Deal with it.

Don't make an issue of it. One idea is to start bedtime stories by sending them to the bathroom. You can get synthetic sheets to lie under the sheets – but they puddle. Do that, but place a couple of bath towels between that and the bottom sheet. In the morning there will be minimal clean up. (Sheets and towels to wash, is all) Please just take it in stride – it happens. I wet the bed when I was young, and there was nothing anyone could do about it then, either – is the way I look at it.

Today you can also get pull-ups for children that can hardly be noticed. If you go that route – get a supply of them – but make the child aware of them in total confidence and then keep them in a place they can get to – but out of sight from everyone else.

Idea 6

START FRESH.

Set a tone early for the quality of the visit.

Make a statement that being together is very important to you. I had a small kitchen table, but every time I had my daughter I had fresh flowers in a jar on the table and a bowl of fresh fruit. I would do that if I had a boy, as well. It's classy – a hotel would do it – and it costs very little for a very positive impression. (Kids usually love grapes and apples and blueberries and small fruit.) Sometimes I would bring the flowers from the store during our - *coming into town stop* - at the grocery, and in the morning I would ask my child to put them in the vase on the table while I made breakfast. This makes a statement of welcome, our time together is beautiful and important to me, and isn't it going to be a great day?

Idea 7

GOOD TO BE HOME.

Set the table.

Fork goes on the left of the plate – big fork next to the plate, little (or salad fork) to the left of the big fork – if you want to get fancy. Knife and spoon go on the right.

And here's a switch. Buy cloth napkins and let that special little person pick out their very own napkin ring at a store so every time they are with you – they know where to sit, and they know that that napkin ring waits for them every time. I would even set the table regardless of whether you are cooking, or just making sandwiches and soup or just bringing in fast food meals.

A visit with Daddy isn't "a camp out at Daddy's house" – it's a visit to their, very own, "other" house.

I think you will see that this can be an easy habit to create, and how more rewarding the time together can be. Give it time. It sure beats everyone eating sitting in front of a television, staring at a screen, and not interfacing.

Idea 8

YOU SET THE EXAMPLE.

Teach saying "please" and saying "thank you".

The next time you are all out in a pharmacy or grocery, everyone can take their time picking out their own favorite "Thank You" cards from the greeting card aisle. Teach the simple courtesy of "Thank You".

If something happens while you are with them or if they tell you something nice that someone did, help them find an address and encourage a thank you note. In this fast paced, electronic world, this very small act, that actually can be fun, can make a quality statement.

This goes for sending birthday cards, as well. One of the regular routines might be... "Anyone you know have a birthday coming – if so, why don't you send them a nice card and surprise them?"

Idea 9

WHERE'S YOUR COMB?

People who say "People have to take me as I am or forget it" are so full of beans.

If we wanted people to take us the way we were, we wouldn't shave or get haircuts or have mirrors. Women wouldn't shave their legs or armpits, and the New York Yankees wouldn't have a dress code policy. Fact is the first impression someone makes of you or anyone is made in 15 – 20 seconds of meeting you, and it usually lasts a lifetime. See to it that personal hygiene habits are managed. Do loads of laundry if dirty clothes pile up. Ask for help in folding them and putting them away. And, just like your Mom and Grandma did to you, see that clothes are neat and straight and the hair is combed before leaving the house. Neatness and self confidence are not a competition or a game of vanity. They are the disciplines that have to be learned, and they establish the basic habits the urchins will thank you for in years to come – habits that will help build their self esteem and self confidence.

These habits aren't cop outs – they're smart.

Idea 10

FAMILY TALKS.

Give the kids something to think about.

Each time, at the beginning of the visitation I would ask my child to give some thought to something we could discuss later. Then, on the day I was returning her to her Mom, we would talk about her thoughts on the subject, I had asked her to think about. It just made me feel like we were connected a little more - even while apart.   It could be something simple to think about like "should we make a blueberry pie or plant something, the next time you come" or was there anything she needed from me to help her with school or should we visit the children's section of the library or go to the park for a picnic next time.

Nothing earth shaking or revolutionary, just conversation. It works for boys and girls.

Idea 11

GAMES, LOTS OF FUN GAMES.

They are not expensive, and they can open up a whole new world for you.

Board games and one-on-one games – not people stuck staring at a television screen or computer games. We're talking *Chutes and Ladders, Monopoly, Checkers.* Twenty minutes at a game aisle in a toy store can fill your imagination and game shelf with great, age appropriate, games that will bond you with laughter, excitement and conversation while you pass the time away.

ANY RULES?

Of course...we play a game only after the game we are finished with is put all back in the box and put back up on the game shelf.

Try to stay ahead of their attention spans. Plan to play the game for an hour or so and then have your lunch or activities planned, organized and ready to go. Good spontaneity is best achieved when alternatives are planned and organized in advance.

Idea 12

SIMPLE AS A,B,C.

You write the little one on occasion... not a text...not an email...you sit down and handwrite a one or two page letter at regular intervals.

Just talk. Say how you are, talk about the house, just talk about how proud you are of how they are growing and how you can't wait to see them again. Maybe include a happy snapshot you took during a visit.

Now put a stamp on it, and drop it in the mail. You just may have made someone's day a whole lot brighter. Do it every week.

Idea 13

LIFETIME MEMORIES

Come up with a table top *"tree"* of some sort – maybe 2 or 3 foot tall that you could put out of the way until visit times.

Consider having this tree decorated for each and every season as a project. Imagine it with hearts for Valentines time, colorful Easter eggs decorations for Easter, Halloween decorations for Fall, Pilgrim hats for Thanksgiving, etc. On Thanksgiving week redecorate it with handmade ornaments and cut out Christmas decorations. Father's Day pictures of their Dad – on Mother's Day – pictures of their Mom.

This will make the *"tree"* at Daddy's something they will look forward to all year long. It will have meaning and it will make memories. And when the art is being created, be sure you are right there at their side lending a hand – some glue or scissors and ideas as needed. Don't take over – just lend a hand.

Idea 14

BOTH GIRLS AND BOYS LIKE TO COOK OR BAKE!

Pies are so easy. (Except pumpkin – that takes a little more effort) read the can, it will tell you how.

Anyone can buy an already baked pie... only a special Dad can bake one with that special one's help.

1. Buy rolled up pie dough. (Ask your grocer – they will enjoy helping a "Dad" out)
2. Buy 1 or 2 pie tins.
3. Get a small bag of flour – more for atmosphere than need.
4. You already have a rolling pin.
5. Go to the baking aisle and get pie filling cans... (That's right...they come in cans). Get your choice of Apple, Blueberry or whatever they have.

Let your helper pick.

Then – for that special hour or two – you just ask for help in baking a pie. You have the pie tin and dough ready and you watch the magic of what accomplishment can make.

Help out in small ways, of course – but just be there to watch memories in the making.

Idea 15

PLAY SCHOOL.

Actually sit on the floor in their space and be at their beck and call to play school or any other game of their choosing. They like being the teacher, of course. Maybe get a chalk or marker board and put it down at their level.

My child liked to play store, as well. We set up a counter. I would go and shop there. I would ask for a can of peas and some celery and so forth. It was good fun...at a young age level.

Idea 16

YUM.

Macaroni and Cheese can be a lifesaver, but you can make it even better by trying some different variations with it:

1. Get a small can (not a big can) of green peas – drain them and add them whole to the macaroni and cheese after it is done cooking and ready to serve.
2. (Or) Drain a can of tuna and add that.
3. (Or) Boil a couple of hot dogs – cut them up in sections and add them.

Idea 17

IT'S A SNAP.

Get some disposable cameras and leave them around so that magic moments can be captured by all. These will be priceless in years to come when everyone is looking back on these happy and quality times together.

Idea 18

TAAADAAAA!

Learning to cook doesn't mean you have to be a chef.

Just get some ideas on simple meals and plan out a visit in terms of meals in advance. You may surprise yourself on how organized you become and how warm you can make the home by being able to "throw something together". Remember, they are at your house – one of their homes. They are not "camping out or roughing it" - they are at their other house. They don't care if it's one room or a castle. It's their other house – where their Daddy lives.

Idea 19

OWNERSHIP

Consider giving your child their own space...literally.

If you have a room they can call their own, give it to them. Don't double it as a guest room or someone else's room. Make it theirs and theirs alone. If you don't have a spare room, give them a corner, a desk, a table or a drawer in a cabinet – so long as it is all theirs.

Hands off to everyone else! They will take ownership and responsibility for it and will have a sense of belonging – rather than just being an overnight guest.

Idea 20

ALWAYS UNPACK AND PUT AWAY.

Letting your child work out of a suitcase doesn't give a message of permanence.

Make one of the first routines – opening the bag, putting everything away, and putting the bag in the hall closet. When it's time for them to go, give their Mom the same courtesy. Repack the suitcase with clean neatly folded clothes. I promise this will make positive impressions on everyone.

Idea 21

LEARN BROWSING.

Browsing can ease anxieties with children.

If you are going to a store or a souvenir shop or anywhere where a little one can pick something out for themselves; I found it a lot more fun and less disappointing when I said,

"We will be here awhile so make a list of everything you like before you just pick something up and we buy it. We do all the buying at the end of our visit - not before or during."

This way once they have made their list they can select the one or two things – by their own priority - that fits into the budget. I found this a nice way to teach the patience of looking around and also the responsibility of making a decision.

Whatever they chose, it was from a list of things they wanted in the first place, and the decision was theirs. If you were at a place quite awhile, browsing can be great fun.

Making the buying decisions at the end of the day can be even more fun.

Spend the entire day just enjoying each other and the adventure.

Idea 22

JUST DO IT!

Don't be afraid of doing a lot of things badly.

Bowl badly. Cook some things badly or make sandwiches badly. Go fishing with cane poles and bobbers instead of boats and rigs. Play Monopoly badly. Lose at Checkers. Pretend you enjoy "Go Fish". Play catch badly, or shoot baskets badly.

I can give you one certainty from experience. Little ones make their Dads heroes and super human with very little encouragement.

Doing simple things will make lasting impressions. If we all waited for that perfect moment or for the perfect tools or for the perfect training to do something, we would do nothing- ever. Trying is what's perfect.

If you can boil an egg, you are a cook. If you can put a worm on a fish hook, you are a fisherman. If you can lift a bowling ball, you are a bowler. If you can sit on the floor and deal the cards, you are a Dad and a hero for life.

Don't look now, but you are making memories with everything you at least try to do.

There's no such thing as a bad memory when a Daddy tries.

Oh! Remember the flour I told you to get when you all made cookies or pies – even though you may not need it? Well you do need it. Puff some on your faces for the goofy picture you take with the kiddo while you're baking.

Idea 23

SEND THEM HOME WITH SOMETHING.

Now listen to this – it will take some thought, and an open mind.

A holiday is coming, right? You're going to bake something or cut something out, right?

Well consider baking that extra pie or that additional batch of cookies that the little one can take home.

Yes, it is their other home – for their other home. They have two homes now – maybe two pies or enough cookies for two homes sends a good message to their precious brains that everything is cool – we're doing the best we can.

Idea 24

DON'T FORGET THE...

With the kiddo, make two of these before Thanksgiving or Christmas and send one home with the little one.

Don't think about it.

PECAN PIE RECIPE THAT IS BEST IN TOWN

First buy two 9 inch pie shells at the grocery store. Then buy a package of pre made pie dough in the refrigerator section. Help your helper put the dough in the pans and squeeze and pinch the top around the edge of the pans. You can use any knife and go around the edge of the pan and cut the excess dough.

(For 2 pies – double everything below)

4 eggs
¼ teaspoon salt
¼ cup melted butter
1-1/4 cups of Karo light corn syrup
1-1/4 cups of firmly packed brown sugar
1 teaspoon vanilla extract
1 unbaked 9-inch pie shell
1 cup chopped pecans

Beat the eggs with a fork. Add everything else and mix well. Pour this into your pie shell. Now you can either sprinkle the top with pecans or get a lot of whole pecans and lay them all over the top of the pie. They will float if you do it very carefully. Preheat your oven at 350*. Bake at 350* F - 45 to 50 minutes.

Remove from the oven and put on a safe place to cool before you refrigerate it.

I promise this will make you feel good.

Idea 25

MMMMMMMM.

You will be amazed what personal pillows will do for a little one – boy or girl, especially if you make an adventure out of it and let them pick out their own pillow.

I'm talking about a pillow of their very own, not a house pillow. One they will sleep with – and sit on to watch movies, and hug while they're listening to you read them bed time stories, and ones that you make up yourself.

Go to a store and have a "squeeze" test and a squeeze test party. Make sure you explain the difference between foam filled and feather filled, and encourage them to understand the difference of both kinds. Once decisions are made, get their pillow its own special pillow case. That pillow always gets very special care and is put away until its little friend comes next time. Having them put it away and bringing it down each visit would be a good routine.

This will mean a lot to the little one.

Idea 26

LIGHTS, CAMERA, POPCORN.

Let's talk some magic memory time.

My secret for having a great memory time is watching a movie that no one would ever even know to watch or think about. A step out of time or a step back in time – kind of like not liking old things but then surprising ourselves by having a great time in a museum seeing all there is to learn. I found there are some movies that are *ageless* – movies with adventure and movies with humor. Anyone can watch the latest and the greatest – what memory is there in that? The others are the most fun for kids.

Make a ton of popcorn and your favorite Kool Aid or Sunny D and consider one of these.

My Top picks of all time movies to share with kids. *(Add your own – but no fair picking recent releases)*

- Father Goose
- The Great Race
- Home Alone
- Fly Away Home
- Homeward Bound
- She Wore A Yellow Ribbon
- The Black Stallion
- Sandlot
- A Christmas Story
- The Magnificent Men In Their Flying Machines
- Summer Stock
- Grease
- War Games

Go rent one of them – or buy them. No fanfare – no discussion. My movie rule is like my food rule.

My food rule is you have to try everything served...to be polite.

Movie rule – you have to watch the first 10 minutes.

It will work every time. You will be surprised what watching an entertaining movie that you wouldn't normally pick out and they never heard of will do for the fun of the moment. And a "classic" can be watched time and time again.

The popcorn will taste better – I promise.

Idea 27

PLAN A MINI VACATION – AN ADVENTURE.

You will be amazed at how many museums or attractions there are within a couple hour drive from where you are.

(Go to yellowpages.com and put in your city and ask for *museums*) Plan a day trip or an over-night trip, and go see another world from another time. Go share an experience together – one that tells a story and takes you out of the everyday grind.

There are some tremendous museums everywhere. Find them, and plan that picnic or that adventure journey.

If you have a special long weekend, don't waste it hanging around the house. Plan an adventure in advance – food, driving time and everything. Don't forget souvenir t shirts and don't forget to take pictures.

And yes, there will be another dad or two everywhere you go who will be happy to take pictures of you and yours with your camera – and, of course, you would oblige them by returning the favor.

Idea 28

WILL PICASSO, PLEASE RAISE YOUR HAND?

Kids can never have enough crayons, coloring books, paints or craft materials.

Find a local craft store and go there as an adventure – browse it for an hour or so. Remember the "browsing" rules. Watch the little one's eyes light up. Start small, but ask the store manager when they have big sales, and ask if they have any special classes for kids on weekends. It may even open a new world of adventure for you.

Idea 29

HEADS UP.

I'm only going to mention this one time, and I will never bring it up again.

One year, I sent my child's Step Dad a Father's Day card and wrote in it "thank you for being a good Step Dad". That's all I will say about it, but I wouldn't have said it if I was sorry I did it.

Idea 30

MAGIC MEAT.

I will give you a recipe now that:

1. Can be meatballs
2. Can be a meatloaf
3. Be mixed with noodles
2 pounds of hamburger meat.
1 onion chopped
2 raw eggs
2 cups of bread crumbs
4 tablespoons of garlic seasoning

Mix with your hands in a bowl - then

1. For Meatballs - roll into meatballs and pan fry at low heat (Pour some spaghetti sauce over them.

2. For Meatloaf – pack the mixture into a bread baking pan. Ask someone at the meat counter how long and at what temperature.
3. Mixed with noodles – cook in a skillet while you boil some elbow macaroni in a pot. When the macaroni is done, drain it and dump them into the skillet and mix.

Easy – feel good – and they will always remember. And no...it's not too much garlic. Garlic makes a kitchen smell like home.

Idea 31

LET IT ALL HANG OUT!

Don't let pictures or snapshots gather dust.

Whenever you are in a Walgreens or a Dollar Store walk past the picture frame aisle. Grab a couple of frames on sale – small ones for snapshots. Then pick out a couple of your favorite photos and slide them in.

Idea 32

FISHING FOR BOOKWORMS.

During a visitation, find a great big bookstore somewhere, and go browse it for an hour or so or more.

Chances are you can get a coffee or a hot chocolate there, and chances are that there is a children's section that will give everyone a lot of great ideas for future adventures. Join a library! Ask if they have "story telling" on weekends.

Idea 33

FIRST THINGS FIRST...ALWAYS.

Get a special calendar for visitation dates – but as importantly, get a calendar for all other "first" dates or "Very Important" dates.

A religious event like a First Holy Communion; or a Bar Mitzvah; or a Confirmation; or a first day of school; or a graduation; or an awards night.

You have a busy schedule? Don't we all – but we always seem to make room according to our priorities. I drove 5 hours to see a First Communion, spent 45 minutes with the coffee and cupcakes for families following the services, and then drove 5 hours home.

Of course you can do it – Thomas Jefferson rode a horse from Charlottesville to Philadelphia and John Adams rode a horse from Boston to Philadelphia nearly every few weeks or so just to build a nation. Certainly

you can spare a few hours to build a family –
and leave memories forever after.

Idea 34

ALWAYS A "HELLO". ALWAYS A "GOOD BYE"

For everyone, no matter who they are,
always.

No grunts or mumbles...no silent waves.
No matter whom it is at the door when you
are picking up your family or dropping them
off, always extend a hand, shake it and say
hello, and then say good-bye.

You have just risen above it all, and this will
resonate in minds and hearts – though you
may not be aware for a time – but it will.

Don't think about it – do it

Idea 35

KEEP SOME THOUGHTS TO YOURSELF.

An actor playwright once told me tongue-
in-cheek – "Man cannot stoop so low as to
not get the love of a woman or a dog". I did
find this funny, but I explain it in a way to make
such an important point to you.

A Daddy or Mommy cannot be brought down so low as to not receive the total love and absolute adoration of their child – a child's love is unconditional.

So please stay on the mountain. Derogatory statements of any kind about others serve absolutely no purpose – why waste your quality time with them?

Please don't.

One time I actually wrote and had a custom sweatshirt made that said, *"When I Grow up I Want to Marry a Bum just Like My Daddy!"* It was never worn, (right side out, anyway) but it was giggled at for the longest time and it put everything in perspective in a way – without saying a word. It made the point that "this too shall pass," and we got on with quality times never looking back once.

Idea 36

LOL

Develop a quality family sense of humor.

A secret I use in story telling is that good humor is about funny things or situations – bad humor, to me, are "gotcha" things or things where someone (the good guy, anyway) is hurt physically or emotionally and people laugh at it. I try to set that example in my bedtime stories. Keep it simple.

Idea 37

I DIDN'T KNOW THAT!

Remember this. You can buy a cake mix.

You can buy your baking pan. You can buy cupcake liners. You can buy a cupcake baking pan. A cake mix box will make either – a cake or the cupcakes. You choose. Some people don't know this – that's why I'm telling you.

And kids love to ice cupcakes and put sprinkles on them.

Idea 38

WRITE YOUR OWN BEDTIME STORIES.

Just make notes about things that happened in your life that were interesting or fun and even embarrassing…where no one was hurt.

Just come up with a beginning, middle and end. You will get the hang of it, in time.

Some may go a minute or two, but some will go longer.

And when they ask you to repeat them – and they will – you will stretch them as more of the detail comes into your head. Practice your story telling techniques with books of bedtime stories – then try some of your own.

My first attempt ever at making up a bed-time story was when my daughter was four and a half. I was making up my own version of *Goldilocks and the 3 Bears*.

"Once upon a time Goldilocks came down stairs and yelled – "Hey Ma! – I'm going to ride my bike to Seven-Eleven – you need anything?"

My daughter fell on the floor holding her sides giggling, and it wasn't long into the story that she joined in telling the story.

I said:

"and then Goldilocks sat in the little baby chair - Kachunk! Crash! - it was broken and shattered into a million splinters."

"Firewood!" my daughter shouted out.

Then I fell on the floor giggling.

Idea 39

LET THEM MAKE THEIR MARK.

Pick a doorway – pick a wall – it could be the front of the refrigerator (if you own it).

Every visit measure their height in their stocking feet and proudly mark the wall accordingly. Don't forget to write their name and the date and time right next to the mark.

You might consider nailing a painted piece of wood somewhere just for this purpose. When they have stopped growing, take it down and give it to them as a keepsake.

Idea 40

TOP SECRET

This recipe that will make you a hero and keep everyone else asking how on earth you did it.

My Mom and Dad taught me this.

Buy a can of ***sweetened condensed milk (look at the label – get condensed - not evaporated)*** (Buy 4 in case you love the recipe)

DO NOT OPEN OR PUNCTURE THE CAN. Put the can in the bottom of a deep soup or spaghetti pot so you will be able to cover it with water. You can take the paper label off or not. Cover with water so that the water is 3 inches above the can.

Bring the water to a boil and then simmer steadily for four (3) hours so be patient.

WARNING: You must constantly check to be sure that the water is well over the can, because if you don't they can overheat and explode – and it did when I did it wrong one time, when I was young. By the way, you can boil more than one can at a time.

After 3 hours, turn the heat off and get a ladle or tongs or something and take the can(s) out and place them on a rack to cool. Use an oven rack if you don't have anything else. After they are cool, refrigerate them. Then, when they are cool, sit around a table. Open a can, and get a spoon for everyone. You are all about to know what heaven is – one spoonful at a time.

When you get really good at it, you can open both ends of the can and slide it out and slice it. But go with the spoons on the first batch. Even put it on ice cream.

Idea 41

ALONE TIME.

Your children are your children – no one else's.

I learned the awkward way when I made some assumptions that I won't make public here, but all I can suggest is that if your child asks to speak with you "alone," respect their wish and make "alone" possible for a private meeting. Don't embarrass your child by talking about personal matters in front of your friends until you know for a fact that your child is at ease. You won't know that until your child tells you in private that they are. I've learned that the child will say what or whom of your friends they are comfortable or uncomfortable talking around and with the degree of acceptance of those "other people" in their lives. Be patient and try not to push things on them. Respect their wishes for private moments with you at times.

Idea 42

RESPECT THE RULES.

If there is dialogue between parents, discuss rules for movie ratings, bed times, and any other areas that should be discussed.

But here is the hard part. If there is no dialogue between parents, respect the rules on these issues out of a respect for your child and to send the right message.

Don't make your house (their other house) a safe house from any of the rules that are fundamentally sound.

A friend of mine, at 39, told me that when she turned 30. (The age her parents were when she started going from one of her homes to another), she remembered that they (at the same age she was now) totally acted like children during that period of her life.

Stay calm – stay cool – don't be an antagonist on some pretty basic good rules.

Idea 43

LANGUAGE (BAD)

Watch it and correct it if it is abused. Take the high road with language, choice of words and phrases. Set the example and encourage the same.

Idea 44

CONSIDER YOUR COMPASS.

I acquired my compass early on which served me well throughout my child's growing up years. I made a promise to always tell my child the truth – always. This certainly acted as a compass for me throughout a lot of years, and it felt good. It would make me think twice before making decisions, because I would have to tell the truth if asked, by her, about the decisions.

I make it a major point in my bedtime stories that they are all based on some truth that happened to me, and then I take great liberties, of course, in exaggerating them where I can. Kids like the truth. It's more believable, and when you exaggerate the truth – as they hope you do - it can be funnier than made-up stories. I have some whoppers.

Idea 45

LESS IS BETTER…NONE IS BEST.

How do you answer questions about "your situation" to a little one?

I'm not one to give you this advice. I can only share with you my experience. When mine was twelve, I told her that I would like to write a book of the stories I told her through the years and asked her opinion and whether I should use real names in that book.

It was one of our "think" questions. I will only tell you her reply and let you make of it what you will. She said, "Sure Daddy – and you can use names - but only if you promise you won't ever use the "D" word in it." (divorce)

There is a fact, I'm certain, about current "situations."

Whatever it is, it's what it is. They just don't like dwelling on it or talking about it.

There ain't no amount of explaining or conjecture that is going to change it. So I wouldn't try. Just get about building quality time.

Idea 46

TAKE MY DAD'S PLEDGE:

Every boy becomes a man. Any man can become a father, but to be "Dad" takes complete selflessness and total commitment.

Be a Dad.

1) I promise to understand the difference between being a friend to my child and being their Dad. They need me as a Dad – not as a friend.

2) I promise never to abuse the Dad and child responsibility by using negative words, reflections, insinuations, or deeds toward anyone else – at least in their presence.

3) Absolutely, any child of mine can have their personal framed pictures of any and all of their "family" or extended family members they'd like to have in their space in this, their other house.

4) "We all have times in our lives that we can't even begin to explain our personal situation to our own selves. Why on earth would we try to explain it to a child? I promise never to try without counseling by a professional.

5) I promise to keep a steady routine and a table set. I know this is all they want.

6) I will read bedtime stories. I will try to act them out. When I get confident, I will make some up. I've got no time to waste on "stuff". There are too many

adventures to experience and so many things to see and learn.

7) I promise to listen.

Idea 47

TIME FOR A "METAPHOR".

Pretend you're on the Titanic, at sea, and it has hit the iceberg and is sinking and starting to tilt up and turn sideways.

You're thinking:

"This cannot be good," and you jump into a life boat and there is a chance for you to be saved.

Then, you look out in the water and see your child struggling to stay afloat off in the distance and trying to swim towards the life boat.

Would you say?

"Hi sweetie – you're not going to believe it. The captain really screwed up. This big ship we were on left England some time ago with a lame brained pilot and steward, and while we were having our dinner meal (by the way the roast beef was cold so that has to be the chefs fault, but the asparagus was divine. Did you get to try the dessert?) - then, you won't believe, the boat began to rock, and I fell out of my seat (the chairs were quite nice. Did you get to notice them? But the waiter was surly and wouldn't enunciate his words) blah, blah, blah... blah, blah, blah...

Or would you say:

"Here - grab Daddy's hand – let me pull you to safety."

Always be there with a helping hand.

Just shut up and be there for them. This is about them – not about you.

That alone will say a whole lot.

Idea 48

ALLOWANCE.

You might consider finding out what the child's mother would consider a proper allowance. You then might consider sending half of that to the mother for distribution. This is separate and apart from required payments. This is a personal gesture from Dad.

Idea 49

UP, UP AND AWAY!

Live in a room? An apartment? A condo? A house?

Build a tree house. No fooling. Did you ever have a fort when you were young? If you have a tree of your own you can do it, but if you are limited in space I got news for you. You can still do it. If you make pilings of three or four high plastic milk crates obtained from a grocer – the kind that connect when they are stacked – you have the perfect foundation to hold up a half sheet of plywood off in a corner somewhere. Rig a tent or a blanket *lean-to* over it. You will be amazed at the fun it can give a child. Be prepared to sit on the floor nearby to listen, because you will be needed to be their ears on the ground or their "go-to guy."

Above all, be patient.

Idea 50

WHAT'S UP DOC?

Doctor...Dentist...Emergency Room.

Have them all clearly thought out, with contact information located, both on your refrigerator door, and in your wallet – just in case. You might even go to each and personally say hello to the doctor and dentist, tell them your visitation schedule, and ask them if you can bring the little one(s) by just to say hello so they'll be more comfortable if there is a need. That way they wouldn't feel like strangers in a strange place.

Idea 51

WHAT'S NEW?

Don't go crazy, but see if there is an interest that your child has.

Consider ordering a magazine subscription in their name, something wholesome, of course in their name. A subscription that would be mailed to their house with you – something they could anticipate and look forward to, when they came. Of course, they could take it with them when they returned to their other house. Keep it simple. Nothing controversial. Use common sense. Always age appropriate, of course. This would be a nice, and not costly "I love you" gesture from their Dad.

Idea 52

GAME FACE!

The statistics are staggering about what not having a Dad in their lives can do to a child.

As repetitive as it may seem, it's important. It's not about whether a Dad lives with the child or not. It's about the Dad being there emotionally for them as their Dad.

I have a theory – as a Dad.

I'm not a doctor or a therapist - only a Dad - but I think a Dad can condition themselves to survive any change in their lives as a natural order of things. My theory though – and it is my theory only - is that what we may tend to do with a big change – okay a crisis - of this sort is we tend to engage in *hysterics and trauma*. We sometimes "traumatize" *ourselves* and *others* we are in contact with, with our depression, uncertainty and carrying on.

My theory is that, if you can do the very best you possibly can to stay up high on the mountain, be brave enough to stay calm and move on with your life (especially when it's visiting time, at the very least) without dwelling on or verbalizing and revisiting the trauma of your situation, again and again, to the wrong ears, you will be sainted, my friend – as a truly great Dad.

Please try.

Idea 53

LITTLE GIRL'S TALK.

You have to consider the proper time to have a discreet chat with a little girl as they approach puberty. Also whether you know the mother has had the talk or not – which they most likely have. Girls have certain needs. Daughters need to be able to count on Dads when they are visiting or traveling with them.

Like those special times of the month.

My approach was a little stuttering and stammering, but I was positive about wanting to be a responsible dad and to be there for her - just in case. I started by asking her if she and her Mom ever talked about certain, *girl things* - that there may be a time that she may need things. Thank goodness, she interrupted me with a slight grin on her face and informed me that only one girl in her class hadn't started her period yet. She knew exactly what I was alluding to. I asked if it was her, and she said no, so I just very matter of fact, told her that if she ever needed me to run an errand for her to get anything that I would.

It was that short and sweet. I felt good, I didn't have to worry about that and I think she felt good that she would never be uncomfortable or embarrassed asking her dad to run that errand, if the time came.

Idea 54

HOTEL STAYS.

Sometimes you will be traveling or sharing a hotel room for the weekend. I always got two king or queen beds and let all the other rules of privacy etiquette apply. A hotel room is both of your homes away from home.

Don't make it a campout.

Unpack and do everything you would at home. Remember, a visit to Daddy's is just going to their other house – not a vacation.

Idea 55

My prayers are with you.

ADDED NOTE TO GRANDPARENTS

FACTS OF LIFE.

A marriage is about a couple and their in-laws.

When this couple adds children to the mix, everything changes. It is no longer about a couple and their in-laws, any more.

With children a marriage is now, for the first time, a *family* and the couple become parents and the in-laws become *grandparents*.

There is a reason grandparents are not called "grand-laws" and they're not called "grand-ins."

They're called grand<u>parents</u>.

Got it?

Now I'm not going to play dumb – I know when it comes to being there for your own blood, decisions can be a whole lot simpler – in your mind - or at least your instincts can be.

But when children are involved we are wise to slow down a bit – after all, it's not our blood anymore – it's just partly our blood.

The less there is of our blood in an offspring – the bigger our responsibilities become, as caretakers, it would seem. I'm even of a nature that when adoption is in the equation the same holds true – times two.

Now enough about talking about grand parenting like it's a chemistry class...let's get down to basics.

Idea 56

HUH?

To me, a wonderful grandparent – during delicate times is a good teddy bear...they are always there for the kids, and always with a steadfast and reliable warm hug and they just smile and play dumb.

Idea 57

CHILDREN'S WARNING LABEL.

You know how we will sometimes wet our finger and touch quickly on a hot surface of something – like an iron - to measure its temperature? During transitions, kiddos may sometimes do that with grandparents with words – not to see the temperature – but to test to see which way the wind is blowing (about their Dad or Mom) and if there are sides being taken...if you catch my meaning?

Don't buy into it. Rise above it.

They only want teddy bear hugs with no strings attached. Only give them that.

They're crafty at it - so be careful.

Do what my mother would do. I grew up with five brothers and two sisters and if any of us would scream down the stairs that one of the others was killing another she would respond, "That's nice, dear don't fight." We could shout "Mom, Richard tore the pages out of my book and Paul has a can of gasoline in his bed and Mike wants to jump out the window", and she would answer up "That's nice dear, don't fight".

My guess is that kids will probe just to test the water, but they don't really want to know. They just want to know they have a safe haven from stress. They just want their teddy bears hugs and to have a quality good time – with no complications or controversy.

Idea 58

ONCE UPON A TIME...

Read this *Handbook for Weekend Dads* often, and be supportive. Always be polite. Always smile. Read stories.

Idea 59 & 60

Be Teddy Bears.

THE END
& a promise to Worley, kept.

January

Start celebrating Groundhog Day (Go to the Zoo) Too cold? (Visit some pet stores – pretend they're a zoo – but no buying) (Go to a park and take pictures of animals – birds and squirrels)

Prepare for Valentine Day(Bake heart shaped cookies one time) (Drawing paper heart cutouts another time) (Learn to Dance)

February

Start celebrating Valentine Day(Bake cookie hearts one time) (Drawing paper heart cutouts another time) (Learn to Dance) (buy and mail Valentine cards)

March

Start celebrating St. Patrick's Day(Bake cookie shamrocks – with a green food coloring in dough one time) (Shamrock paper cutouts another time)

Start celebrating Easter(Bake cookie Easter eggs one time) (Cookie Easter Bunnies another time)

April

More Easter(Bake cookie Easter eggs)
(Bake cookie Easter Bunnies) (Easter egg coloring) (Easter egg decoration cutouts)(bowling, fishing)

May

Start celebrating Mother's day (C'mon –
be a hero – help design card – wrap a gift –
from them not you) (bowling, fishing)

June

Start celebrating Father's day - Let someone make breakfast and give their Daddy breakfast in bed. (Baseball games) (bowling, fishing)

4th of July Draw and color flags – Put out a flag. Find a picnic or fireworks display.

July

Picnics – Swimming – Library visits – Fishing – Croquet – Zoo – Baseball games – July 4th fireworks shows – museums. (Baseball games) (bowling, fishing)

August
Picnics – Swimming – Library visits – Fishing – Croquet – Zoo – Baseball games – museums. (Baseball games) (bowling, fishing)

September

Start celebrating Pre Halloween(Bake cookie pumpkins and Halloween cookie shapes) (or Halloween paper cutouts) (Baseball games) (bowling, fishing)

October

Start celebrating Halloween (Cookie pumpkins and Halloween cookie shapes) (paper pumpkin and cat cutouts) (Go to a pumpkin lot and get pumpkins to carve)

Start celebrating Pre Thanksgiving(Cookie holiday shapes – Christmas or Pilgrim hats) (Paper cutouts)

Decorate a "Family Christmas table tree – with decorations drawn, colored and cut out.

November

Start celebrating Thanksgiving(Bake cookie holiday shapes – Christmas or Pilgrim hats) (Paper cutouts) (Put up a small Christmas tree – and start decorating with cutouts (and lights)

Start celebrating Christmas(Bake cookie Holiday shapes – Christmas stars and candy canes and snowmen) (paper cutouts)

December

(Cookie Holiday shapes – Christmas stars and candy canes and snowmen, paper cutouts)